G000134783

"At 3:37 A.M. on a Sunday, I frantic phone call from a new Macintosh. She had gotten her en ly out of the house and was calling neighbor's. I asked her why on earth she had evacuated her house in the middle of the night. Turns out she had just received her first system error. She interpreted the little picture of a bomb as a warning that the computer was about to blow up. . . "

Go into the trenches of tech support— and discover some of the wildest, weirdest, and funniest calls the computer experts have ever received. From fax failures to software screwups to disk debacles, the most hilarious stories are here in . . .

TALES from the Tech Line

Also Edited by David Pogue

The Great Macintosh Easter Egg Hunt
The Microsloth Joke Book

TALES from the TECH LINE

edited by DAVID POGUE

BERKLEY BOOKS,
NEW YORK

This book is an original publication of The Berkley Publishing Group.

TALES FROM THE TECH LINE

A Berkley Book / published by arrangement with the editor

PRINTING HISTORY
Berkley trade paperback edition / June 1998

The Penguin Putnam Inc. World Wide Web site address is
http://www.penguinputnam.com

ISBN: 0-425-16363-6

BERKLEY®
Berkley Books are published by The Berkley Publishing Group, a member of Penguin Putnam Inc., 200 Madison Avenue, New York, New York 10016. BERKLEY and the "B" design are trademarks belonging to Berkley Publishing Corporation.

PRINTED IN THE UNITED STATES OF AMERICA

10 9 8 7 6 5 4 3 2 1

FOREWORD

Over twelve years ago, I worked for a small publisher in upstate New York who bought a Macintosh computer for our office. None of us knew much more than how to use it as a glorified typewriter.

I silently claimed ownership as I tapped the keys with both index fingers and happily shoved plastic shingles in the open slots in the front. Suddenly, I loved my job.

But the day I was to send our first computer-generated catalog to the film house, the unthinkable happened: The machine would not start. I had no idea why there was a flashing question mark on the screen, but I knew this couldn't be a good thing.

I called the retailer's technical support line and frantically explained my situation. I was told, "Your computer is suffering from disappearing hard drive."

< V >

"Oh, no! How do I get it back?"

The tech vaguely explained this common, yet serious problem and suggested I overnight the hard drive to him. He walked me through the process of opening the case and removing the big metal brick that held my life's data. In the process, I noticed a dozen or so missing floppy disks scattered across the motherboard. All of this was a monumental learning experience, even if I learned only that that's where all the diskettes go when you stick them into a slot that has no floppy drive under the hood.

The retailer fixed the hard drive after discovering that I had installed six duplicate operating systems. The drive was shipped back to us, and the catalog files went off to the printer successfully.

Today I work in the information-technologies field; I've come a long way since the days when I could hose a Macintosh like nobody's business. I still think about my humorous actions back then, and applaud every customer who has ever used the mouse as a foot pedal or interpreted the CD-ROM tray as a cup holder. Not only have these understandable gaffes brought a few laughs into the workplace, but the individuals behind the keyboard often display a certain common sense and willingness to forge fearlessly ahead. After all, it's just a computer, and you can always pull the plug.

Eric Hausmann
Editor, *Tech Support Tales*

< vi >

Foreword

Eric Hausmann's *Tech Support Tales* is a Web zine that compiles humorous true stories from the world of computer technical support. Eric's E-mail address is hausmann@ohsu.edu, and the *Tech Support Tales* Web site is located at http://www.auricular.com/TST.

< vii >

TALES from the TECH LINE

INTRODUCTION

About 45 percent of Americans today own a personal computer; the rest don't know how lucky they are.

No matter how fast these machines become, or how powerful, or how "user-friendly" (ha!), the list of things that can go wrong just gets longer and longer. In fact, one study shows that when you factor in the time we spend fiddling with Windows, trying to make our CD-ROMs work, installing new printers, and so on, we're actually *less* productive than we were before we had the computer!

It's no wonder, then, that in homes and offices nationwide, private dramas unfold daily in the relationships between us and our computers. No one witnesses these quiet battles more clearly than the kindly souls who man the tech-support hotlines at computer companies these days. These men and women fight all day long in the

< xi >

technophobic trenches, on the receiving end of the frustrated callers' emotions; each computer company receives several thousand calls *a day* from frustrated customers.

Over the years, the help-desk reps have collected their favorite stories in private notebooks, passed them on by E-mail, or shared them over pizza and beer. This book contains several hundred of the most hilarious and amazing tech-support tales, from the lady who thought her mouse was a foot pedal, to the guy who tried to fax by holding a page up to the computer screen and pressing the Send key.

These stories come from Internet postings, interviews, and E-mail messages. The largest single source of them is a free Internet-based E-mail newsletter called *Tech Support Tales*; its creator, Eric Hausmann, graciously offered me pilfering rights of his stash. Where possible, I've credited the original storyteller (unless anonymity was requested).

These tales are funny, of course, but they're also enlightening; they make us realize, deep down, that the computer's owners aren't the stupid ones. The real silliness is our effort to create a relationship between our human selves and a $3000 hunk of plastic and silicon. The only fault of the hapless tech-line callers is trying to make sense of it all in the first place.

< xii >

TALES from the
TECH LINE

The Computer

There it sits: a machine you've spent several months' salary on, glowering at you, covered with slits and knobs and jacks and accompanied by a manual apparently translated from Japanese by native Swahili speakers. The commercials have led you to believe that this machine will make you a more efficient, more powerful, and more glorious human being.

If you can get it turned on, that is.

■ ■ ■

It's a New Feature, Ma'am

Tech: Tech support, how may I help you?
Caller: This computer is brand-new, and it doesn't even work.
Tech: Well, ma'am, have you set it up correctly?
Caller: Well, I think so. I unpacked it, set it up, and plugged it

< 1 >

in. But now I've sat here for twenty minutes waiting for something to happen, and it just won't come on.

Tech: Well, what happens when you press the Power switch?

Caller: What Power switch?

■ ■ ■

No, the *Other* CPU

A woman came into our shop and told us that she was having problems with her monitor. We suggested that she bring her monitor in, and we promised to check it out.

She brought in the monitor. We plugged it in. It worked without a flaw. We told her that the monitor wasn't the problem—and we asked her to bring in her CPU.

She stared at us blankly. "What's the CPU?"

"You know," I explained, "it's the central piece of equipment that all your other devices plug into."

I guess I shouldn't have been surprised. She returned an hour later, sure enough, carrying the piece of equipment she plugged everything into.

Her surge suppresser.

< 2 >

■ ■ ■

Talk About "General System Faults"!

It's nice to know that high-tech confusion isn't limited to the civilian population, isn't it? This tale comes to us from the system administrator for an Air Force office.

The Help Desk gave me a call from Major So-and-So, who was having a problem with his workstation. I called him and he told me, "Every time I switch it over to 'Official,' the damn screen goes blank!"

I had no idea what this "Official" switch was, but I was dying to find out. I went down to the major's office.

After nearly getting court-martialed for laughing so hard, I spent about twenty minutes explaining to this ex-pilot that "Off" was not an abbreviation for "Official."

■ ■ ■

Let's Hope It Wasn't Easter

Most computer glitches stem from flaky hardware, flaky software, or flaky users. Occasionally, however, something more surprising can hop up, as this London technician reports.

< 3 >

A customer walked in with a dead PowerBook 165. Problem description: Freezes on startup. An additional symptom: While being carried to our service center, customer says he heard a sloshing noise within the machine.

"Has anything been spilled on this computer?" I inquired. No, no, nothing of the sort, protested the client. Taking this with a grain of salt, I went about filling in the repair order.

On the workbench, I started the PowerBook. Sure enough: An address error on startup, just after "Welcome to Macintosh." I lowered my ear to the keyboard, at which point I heard a crackling noise and became aware of a rather sharp odor. I flicked the computer off and removed the battery from its compartment, only to observe that the entire battery casing was soaked in a clear fluid. I also noticed that the same fluid was leaking out of the battery compartment.

My first thoughts were that the battery had somehow leaked acid, which would account for the sharp smell (which reminded me of ammonia)—yet the battery terminals were dry.

Tipping the machine on its side, I watched more fluid run out onto the bench in a puddle about the size of a compact disc. I then unscrewed the computer and separated the two parts of the PowerBook.

The smell suddenly became a lot stronger. The hard disk looked like a solid lump of rust, and the daughterboard had the appearance of three barbecued chips. I invited several of my workmates in to take a sniff and offer an opinion. We were unanimous in our deci-

< 4 >

sion. I called the customer, who seemed surprised when I asked, "Do you have a cat?"

As it turned out, he didn't have a cat, but he did have a lovely fluffy bunny rabbit, who had been seen in the vicinity of the PowerBook only the day before. Yes, there was no doubt about it, little Fluffy had hopped up onto the keyboard and downloaded some incompatible data.

I checked the warranty form, but there was no provision anywhere for failure due to rabbit urine. I advised the customer to get in touch with his insurance company.

In the end, the PowerBook was unrepairable, and the customer upgraded to a 180c. I cleaned up the static mat and sprayed the service department with a healthy dosage of "Fresh Field of Flowers." I checked in with the customer a week later, asked how was he enjoying the 180c, asked if he'd managed to restore his data. And, of course, I asked how his rabbit was.

"Delicious," he said.

■ ■ ■

Handyman Special

Some computers are designed for easy upgrading when faster processor chips become available; you just pop out the old chip and replace it with the new. Older computers, however, came with un-upgradable

< 5 >

processor chips that were soldered permanently to the main circuit board. Which leads us to this tech-line transcript:

Caller: Where can I get a BIOS upgrade for my 286 computer?

Tech: Hm. Your computer should have been shipped with the latest BIOS.

Caller: Well, I upgraded the processor myself, and now my computer doesn't seem to work.

Tech: What did you upgrade the processor to?

Caller: I upgraded it to a 486DX-50.

Tech: But, sir . . . the 286 chip is soldered on the motherboard!

Caller: I know, but I got it out OK. I used my handy-dandy soldering iron, took out the old chip, and put the 486 on myself.

Tech: Sir, the 486 chip is considerably bigger than the 286!

Caller: Tell me about it. I had to use quite a bit of solder to melt all those extra pins together.

■ ■ ■

Our Lady of Computer Glitches

I am a service tech.

I received a desperate call from a woman about seventy-five miles away. Symptom: The computer was dead—no lights, no display, no

< 6 >

sounds, nada. My first question to this lady was, "Have you verified that it is plugged into a working power outlet?" She was so insulted, she just about ripped my lungs out over the phone.

I jumped into my van and drove the seventy-five miles to this customer's site. As I was getting out of the van, a little voice in my head said, "Leave your tools in the van." So I did.

When I walked in and saw the setup, I saw the problem immediately. The computer was plugged into one of those multi-adapters that let you plug half of your house into a single outlet. It was falling out of the wall, dangling at about a forty-five-degree angle!

The lady was standing there, breathing fire by this time. I laid my hands on top of the monitor and stated loudly, "If you believe in the Lord Jesus Christ, *be healed!*" and at the same time I kicked the plug into the wall while slapping the top of the monitor. Lo and behold, everything went beep, the monitor lit up, and everything was OK. I pulled out my service book, wrote on the ticket "I healed it," and left.

She never called again.

■ ■ ■

Beeps from Hell

One customer kept reporting a problem to us. Over and over again, she would complain that her Mac was beeping at her. The

< 7 >

beeping would happen at the strangest and most random times—sometimes even when nobody was at the computer. This random behavior, of course, made our troubleshooting by phone much more difficult. There wasn't much we could do, other than to ask her to call us the next time the problem occurred.

She did. This time, we were ready. We had her close her windows, quit her programs, and even turn off the Mac. The beeping continued!

From that point, it didn't take long to discover the source of the beeping. Her coworker's pager had been dropped under her desk.

■ ■ ■

Turn Up the User Brightness Knob

I am the systems manager at a large-circulation daily newspaper.

One day, our society editor was typing away at her terminal. As I passed her desk, she asked me to turn up the brightness on the monitor, because it was too dark. As I leaned over to twist the Brightness knob, I noticed that the Power switch was in the off position.

She had been typing her story on a deactivated computer for thirty minutes, and didn't even notice!

< 8 >

■ ■ ■

Step 2: See Step 1

Not every over-the-phone computer mystery is the customer's fault. Every now and then, the technician is involved . . .

Over the phone, we were trying to talk one of our customers through an installation of an SBUS card (a circuit board) in a Sun SPARC-station 20. She carefully followed each of our instructions, removing the top of the machine, swapping RAM chips, moving hard drives, moving SBUS cards around, and so on.

But about halfway through the installation, the customer on the other end of the line commented that "funny things" were happening on her monitor.

Suddenly I realized the problem: We had forgotten to tell her to start by turning off the computer!

■ ■ ■

The Handyman Can

Computer memory comes on small circuit boards—memory modules—called SIMMs. These modules snap into corresponding slots on the com-

< 9 >

puter's main circuit board; when you want to install another SIMM, you simply slip it into an available slot. It's that easy—usually.

I was trying to help a caller who was trying to remove a 4-megabyte SIMM from his Macintosh LC III so he could install an 8-meg SIMM in its place. He complained that he was having trouble with the 4-meg module: It appeared to be soldered in.

I asked him if he had released the SIMM from the clips that hold it in place; he said he'd had to rip the clips completely off. He said the ends of the SIMM module could now wiggle free, but the middle was soldered in. I tried to understand what the hell was going on in his Mac . . . The weirdness went on for at least five minutes. Grasping for some semblance of reality, I asked how much memory his LC III had had originally.

"Four megs," came the reply.

At this moment, the customer looked at his installation instructions again. "Ohhhhh," he said, "you gotta take it out if you have *more* than four megs." He had been ripping the SIMM *slot* out of the computer!

Of course, he asked if he should just solder it back down.

■ ■ ■

If General Motors Had a Help Line, Part I

Tech: General Motors Help Line, how can I help you?

Caller: I got in my car and closed the door and nothing happened!

Tech: Did you put the key in the ignition slot and turn it?

Caller: What's an ignition?

Tech: It's a starter motor that draws current from your battery and turns over the engine.

Caller: Ignition? Motor? Battery? Engine? How come I have to know all these technical terms just to use my car?

■ ■ ■

The World's Worst Mouse Pad

Helping a computer novice over the phone is never easy—and sometimes only a house call will do, as in this case reported by a consultant.

Tech: PC experts, can I help you?

Customer: My computer's acting weird.

Tech: What's happening?

< 11 >

Customer: The little arrow is jumping all over the screen when I move my mouse.

Later, upon visiting the customer's office to see what could be causing the jumping:

Tech: Would you show me how it acts weird, please?

(The customer began using her mouse. Sure enough, the cursor arrow jumped wildly all over the monitor. And no wonder: She was dragging the mouse across the keys of her keyboard.)

■ ■ ■

Caffeine Intolerance

Programmer/analyst Charles T. Brown once handled hardware support for his company. How could he forget this case?

One of our users called to say that his terminal was acting up. "The screen is completely blank," he said, "except for this little dash that keeps dancing around the screen."

I tried everything I could think of over the phone, but to no avail. Upon arriving at the fellow's desk, true to his word, the cursor was dancing around on a blank screen. I tried turning it off, unplugging

< 12 >

it, the works, but nothing seemed to work. I decided I'd have to haul the whole computer back to the shop.

Preparing to pack everything up, I picked up the keyboard—when out of the keys poured the entire contents of the empty Coke can that was sitting on the guy's desk. He turned bright red. "How'd that happen?" he asked sheepishly.

■ ■ ■

Crossing the Restarting Line

Shutting down certain Mac models, as on many Windows machines, involves two steps. First, you choose a Shut Down command; after a moment, when the computer says It's safe to shut down the computer now, *you flip off the Power switch. But that's not how TV sets and light switches work, so some confusion is inevitable.*

The whole family was astonished at how powerful our new Power Mac was. We had been taking turns using it all evening, and at around 10 P.M., everyone started turning in.

Except for Mom, that is. She used the computer for a couple more hours. Then, just before she got up to go to bed, a problem arose. She called Apple's help line.

Mom: Could somebody there please tell me how in the world to

< 13 >

shut down my computer!? I've been trying to shut it down for the past *three hours*!

Tech: You just press the button.

Mom: I've been doing that, and the computer keeps restarting!

Tech: Tell me what you are doing.

Mom: I go to the Special menu, I go to Shut Down, and I release the mouse button. But it doesn't shut down! It just gives me a message that says, *It is now safe to shut down your computer,* with only one button that says Restart, and when I press it, my computer restarts. How do I get it to shut down? It has been restarting for the past three hours!

Tech: No . . . not that button. The little white button in front of the computer. You know, the one you use to turn it on.

Mom: Ohhhhhhh, *that* one!

Mom was very embarrassed. In fact, ever since, whenever she needs any assistance from Apple, she has *me* call them; she thinks that when she gives them her name, they've got the word "idiot" next to it on their database screen.

< 14 >

■ ■ ■

Maybe the Fifteenth One Will Work

A tale from Down Under—from Sydney, Australia, consultant Simon Cousins.

I was recently called into a client's offices to diagnose a supposedly faulty floppy disk drive. There was indeed something amiss—when I poked my first test diskette into the slot, it simply clattered into the chassis. Upon opening the case, I found that the whole floppy disk drive mechanism had been *stolen*.

Inside, where the drive used to be, were a number of floppy disks lying in a heap. My client had simply kept on inserting diskettes until he realized that none of them were showing up on the screen!

■ ■ ■

Well, At Least It's Clean

Tech: Technical Support, may I help you?

Caller: Yeah, my keyboard has stopped working, and I can't figure out why.

Tech: It doesn't work at all?

< 15 >

Caller: Nope. I even cleaned it.

  Tech: You cleaned it?

Caller: Yeah. I soaked it in the tub with soap and water for a day, even took all the keys off and washed them individually. For some reason, it still won't work.

■ ■ ■

The Haunted PC

A client called me in sheer panic. "My computer keeps turning off by itself," she said. Fearing the worst, I went to her office immediately. Once there, I saw that her screen was indeed dark. I also noticed that she wasn't wearing any shoes.

Instinctively, I investigated her surge suppressor—the power strip into which she'd plugged her computer; its master switch was turned off. Immediately nearby was her right shoe, and the whole scenario became clear. Whenever she took a break from typing and stretched her toes, she'd been hitting the power strip's On/Off switch—and cutting off her own power.

< 16 >

■ ■ ■

Color Coordination

Caller: Let's say, just hypothetically, that I wanted to buy a new computer case from you. Could I do that?

Tech: Just the case? No internal components?

Caller: Yeah. Just the plastics.

Tech: Well, it depends. What kind of computer?

Caller: Well, let's say, hypothetically, a Quadra 630.

Tech: Exactly what parts are we talking about?

Caller: Well, let's say, hypothetically, the sides and the top.

Tech: Did this hypothetical machine come without plastic?

Caller: No, this would be in the event of, well, let's say, on the off chance that a small child painted the top and sides of the computer.

Tech: Did this hypothetical child use watercolors?

Caller: Would it be covered under warranty if she didn't?

Tech: Hypothetically, no. You could always buy more paint and paint a more pleasing design over it, though.

< 17 >

■ ■ ■

Debugging

One of our user-types came to our maintenance shop and told me he had a bug in his computer and wanted me to take a look at it. As we walked back to his cubicle, I tried to ascertain exactly what was the problem, but he just kept chattering on about some kind of bug in the system.

When we got to his computer, he lifted the top portion of his keyboard (which he had managed to pry apart) and pointed. Sure enough, there was a cockroach stuck in one of the keyboard springs.

■ ■ ■

You Were Doing 55 MHz in a 40 MHz Zone

Most computer companies like to think that they build sturdy computers, of course, but this . . . ?

This morning, I had a call from a woman who said she was having trouble with the screen on her new computer.

I asked her what she had done, and she said she had *driven over* her machine. I asked her if she *actually* had driven over her com-

< 18 >

puter. She said yes. She explained that the day she received the computer, it was raining. She dragged it from the UPS truck to her garage, where she forgot about it. The next morning, she backed her Jeep over the computer. At this point, the Jeep was stuck—so she put it in four-wheel drive and drove over the computer again.

■ ■ ■

Big Blue, Big Hair

I had a job a few years ago at a major utility company, and this story is legend there.

The company was a Big Blue shop—all IBM equipment. In one of the remote districts, this one branch office's computers went down religiously at 12:30 every day for about thirty minutes. Then everything would come back up.

Everyone was puzzled. The techies worked on the problem from the host site for weeks. IBM was called and they all scratched their heads. Finally, they sent a guy out to the actual remote station to investigate.

It turns out that the controller that ran the computers in that location was installed in an odd way. There was no power available in the closet where the controller was installed. Rather than running an outlet into the closet, the contractor had simply drilled a hole in the wall and plugged the controller into an outlet in the women's rest room.

The daily outage was caused by a noontime exerciser unplugging the controller so she could plug in her hair dryer.

■ ■ ■

Electric Spaghetti

I work as the computer-support tech for a state agency. One day a user called for help. She complained that she had moved her PC to a new desk, and it wouldn't turn on. I asked her the standard questions: Is it plugged in? Is the power strip on? Are all the cables connected? She answered yes to all of them, and I told her I would come take a look at it.

Sure enough, the computer would not power up, so I proceeded to double-check all the cables. I followed the power cord through a jumble of cables to the power strip. The power strip's switch was in the on position, so I followed *its* power cord to see where it led.

Much to my amusement, I found that she had plugged the power strip cord into one of its own outlets.

< 20 >

■ ■ ■

Now Then: What About the Brake?

This tale has become one of the most famous tech stories of all time. We join the story in progress after a new customer has complained that her computer apparently won't do anything. The tech has verified that his customer has set up, plugged in, and turned on the computer correctly.

> *Caller:* I've pushed and pushed on this foot pedal and nothing happens.
> *Tech:* . . . Foot pedal?
> *Caller:* Yes, this little white foot pedal with the On switch.
> *Tech:* The foot—Oh, *that* foot pedal. Ma'am, that's called the mouse. It's meant to be rolled around on your desk.

■ ■ ■

I Think It's Next to the Shift Key

Robert Hook isn't the first to file a report like this—or the last.

< 21 >

I used to work for a company that wrote and sold systems for the agricultural market. I got a call from one of our clients one day. Now, this fellow couldn't have been totally stupid, since he managed a cattle ranch as big as Tasmania. But he was really frustrated with our latest update disk. During the installation, a message told him, *Press Any Key to Continue*—he'd spent over thirty minutes trying to find the Any key on his keyboard.

■ ■ ■

Making Progress

A woman brought her Macintosh into my shop to have more memory installed; she said that the computer kept running out of memory at startup. That was certainly a peculiar report, so I decided to fire up the machine at the counter while she watched.

After plugging in the computer, I hit the Power button. The computer sprang to life and the *Welcome to Macintosh* logo appeared onscreen. Exactly as on any Macintosh, the startup progress bar then appeared, inching its way across the screen to show how much longer the startup process was going to take. As the bar approached the end of its journey, my customer pointed to it excitedly. "See, look!" she said. "The memory is all full!"

I looked at her, confused, and asked where she got that idea. Apparently one of the know-nothings at the local computer super-

< 22 >

store had told her that that was what the progress bar meant. She ending up not buying the RAM, but was thankful for our good service.

■ ■ ■

The San Francisco Low-Crime Program

Caller: Hi. I'm calling about the free computers for people who live in San Francisco area.

Tech: What program is that?

Caller: The program where Apple gives a free computer if you turn in your gun.

Tech: You mean, you turn in a gun, and we give you a computer?

Caller: Yeah.

Tech: —?

■ ■ ■

No, That's Not OK

A customer called us to say that his computer was acting "funny." The customer said that he couldn't understand why his Mac

< 23 >

should be acting up—"After all," he told us, "the Mac says that it's OK!"

That last comment made us wonder. We asked him exactly how the Mac was communicating that it was OK.

"It's right there, at the top of every window" was the reply.

It was then that we realized that the computer actually said "zero K"—the customer's hard drive was completely full!

■ ■ ■

Who Made Your Shopping List, Anyway?

Another transcript from the Apple 800 hot line. The tech rep has just asked the caller which Mac model he has recently purchased.

Caller: Well, it's an Apple computer.

Tech: We make several different computer models, sir. You can find the name on the front of the computer.

Caller: Well, it says Multiple Scan 17 Display.

Tech: OK, sir, that's your monitor. The computer will have its name on the front.

Caller: What do you mean, "computer?"

Tech: The box itself.

Caller: The monitor?

< 24 >

Tech: No, the computer is where you would put a floppy disk and plug in the keyboard.

Caller: I don't have one of those. I think that may be the problem.

Tech: What *do* you have?

Caller: I have a CD-ROM, a monitor, a keyboard, and a printer . . .

■ ■ ■

Maybe Your Pinky's Broken, Too

A customer brought in his computer to our service center, asking to have his Return key fixed.

"All the other keys work fine, just the Return key is broken?"

"Yes," he replied.

Our technician checked out the keyboard. It all worked fine, including the Return key. He came back out to talk to the customer. "It works OK for me," he said. "Can you describe exactly what the problem is?"

"I'm typing in the commands to use it, and everything is just fine until I press the Return key. Then it always prints on my screen: *?? ERROR—FILE NOT FOUND*. I never get that problem until I hit the Return key, so I know that's the key that's bad."

< 25 >

■ ■ ■

We Won't Need the Glue, Then

While talking with a gentleman on the phone who was having problems with a newsletter he had created, we were going through the usual questions. At one point I asked him, "Has your computer crashed lately?"

His reply: "No, it's been sitting right here on the desk the whole time."

■ ■ ■

A Cord by Any Other Name . . .

An Apple rep was helping a customer disconnect peripherals from the back of her machine. Little did he know the conversation was soon to touch upon System 7 (a version of the operating-system software) and HyperCard (a software program included with each Mac).

> *Tech:* OK, what do you have connected to the back of your computer?
> *Caller:* I have a printer, a modem, and the System 7 module.
> *Tech:* Excuse me, but could you repeat the last item?

< 26 >

Caller: The System 7 module.

Tech: The System 7 what?

Caller: It's the module to upgrade the system to 7.5.

Tech: ... And it plugs into the back of your computer?

Caller: Yes.

Tech: Does this "module" plug into anything else?

Caller: It plugs into the wall outlet.

Tech: Ma'am, that's the power cord.

Caller: No, I can see the power cord. *This* module is plugged in right next to it.

Tech: Ma'am, there is no such thing as a System 7 module.

Caller: Oh, my goodness, I'm sorry, you're right. It's actually the power supply to the HyperCard.

Tech: Ma'am, HyperCard does not have a separate power supply. Would you mind following the cord from the outlet until you find what it plugs into?

Caller: OK.

(Tech waits for more than ten minutes.)

Caller: It hooks into the printer.

< 27 >

■ ■ ■

Just Ignore the Shrapnel

I just got off the phone with a gentleman who was extremely pleased with his laptop. He dropped it from a high location in his office onto a hard tile floor, and it literally smashed to pieces. He said the entire unit came apart, with broken pieces everywhere.

Well, he spent a little time putting it back together. He told me he just left the little pieces that were broken or that he didn't recognize in a little pile. He says the machine operates just like new now. He just wanted to call to say how wonderful it is that we make such tough and user-friendly computers.

■ ■ ■

She's Gonna Blow

At 3:37 A.M. on a Sunday, I received a frantic phone call from a new user of a Macintosh. She had gotten her entire family out of the house and was calling from the neighbor's. I asked her why on earth she had evacuated her house in the middle of the night.

Turns out that she had just received her first system error. She interpreted the little picture of a bomb (in the *Sorry, a system error has occurred* box) as a warning that the computer was about to blow up.

< 28 >

The Software

Naturally, the computer can't do anything by itself. Without software, it's nothing more than an expensive doorstop.

Add a state-of-the-art operating system and a suite of modern application software, though, and it's *really* useless.

■ ■ ■

Don't Believe Everything You Read

One customer called tech support because an error message had appeared on his screen, and he couldn't seem to make it go away.

> *Caller:* I'm typing eleven over and over, and the message box
> still won't go away.
> *Tech:* You're what?

< 29 >

Caller: I'm typing 11 on my keyboard. I've done it about a hundred times. The message box still won't go away.

Tech: I'm sorry, sir, I don't understand. Why are you typing 11?

Caller: Well, that's what the message says! It says, *Error Type 11!*

■ ■ ■

Multi-User, Single Brain

Life with computers is always more complicated when "multi-user" systems are involved—databases, for example, that several people on a network can access simultaneously.

I was hired to set up a multi-user 4th Dimension database for a client. For simplicity, I started by setting it up on a single machine. When I left the client's office that day, everything was working fine on that one computer.

But the customer called me back the next day, saying he was very frustrated trying to get the multi-user feature working. "I can't use both machines at once," he said; "the other user keeps messing up the screen."

I was baffled, because I hadn't yet turned on the multi-user op-

< 30 >

tion. Turns out that the client had simply plugged two keyboards into the same computer and thought that meant multi-user.

■ ■ ■

Less Disk for the Money

Appearances can be deceiving, and upgrades can be confusing. Especially if you're the customer of the utility software company whose tech-support agent reported this call.

Caller: You people are cheating me. When I bought your program three years ago, it came on four diskettes. This new version I bought today only has three! Are you cutting back on your program's features, or what?

Tech: No, sir. Actually, the new version has more features than ever before, but now we ship the program out on high-density disks.

Caller: High-density disks? What the hell difference does it matter how much the floppies weigh?

< 31 >

■ ■ ■

The Trash Doesn't Do Windows

A New York City consultant set up a client—a famous screenwriter—with his first Macintosh. After an afternoon of lessons, the screenwriter seemed to be managing fairly well, so the consultant went home.

That evening, however, the screenwriter called in a panic. "I can't throw any goddam thing away!" he shouted into the phone, claiming that no matter how many items he dragged to the Mac's onscreen Trash can, nothing would go in.

The consultant asked all the usual questions. "Are you putting the tip of the arrow directly on the Trash can? Are you letting go when the document is directly over the Trash?" and so on; the answers were all affirmative. Finally, utterly bewildered, the consultant returned to the screenwriter's apartment for a midnight rescue call.

Everything the client had said was true: Indeed, he had tried dragging thirty-five different files to the Trash. The only problem: He had been dragging these document's *open windows*, not their icons, onto the Trash. There, greeting the consultant, were thirty-five windows, all crammed into the lower-right corner of the screenwriter's screen.

< 32 >

■ ■ ■

File-Recovery Software—Now with ESP!

Norton Utilities can rescue saved data from a disk that's gone bad. But one customer complained angrily to a Symantec tech-support agent that the program had been unable to recover the caller's typing—even though the customer had switched off the computer before even saving his work.

■ ■ ■

The Upgrade Paradox

   Tech: Hello, Tech Support.
Caller: Yeah, I've got version 3.1 of your program and it won't run on my Macintosh 7500.
   Tech: Yes, sir, that's right. 3.1 is not compatible with the new PCI Power Macs. You need version 5.0 or later.
Caller: Yeah, well, I've got that version 5, too. Works fine.
   Tech: That's great, sir. So you have the upgrade, then. So what's the problem?
Caller: Well, I just want to know when you're gonna make the

< 33 >

3.1 version run on Power Mac. We've been using the 3.1 version years more than the 5.0, and we like it just fine.

■ ■ ■

If General Motors Had a Help Line, Part 2

Tech: General Motors Help Line, how can I help you?

Caller: My car ran fine for a week, and now it won't go anywhere!

Tech: Is the gas tank empty?

Caller: Huh? How do I know?

Tech: There's a little gauge on the front panel with a needle and markings from E to F. Where is the needle pointing?

Caller: It's pointing to E. What does that mean?

Tech: It means you have to visit a gasoline vendor and purchase some more gasoline. You can install it yourself or pay the vendor to install it for you.

Caller: What? I paid fifteen thousand dollars for this car! Now you tell me that I have to keep buying more components? I want a car that comes with everything built in!

< 34 >

■ ■ ■

Word Imperfect

This report comes from a WordPerfect tech-support rep. File this one under, "So that explains it."

The caller was upset because she could not edit her document. She said she had loaded the document into WordPerfect, and she could see and read the words, but she could not edit the text.

I was puzzled until she told me she had *scanned in* the document. WordPerfect doesn't come with any OCR (optical character recognition) software, so it didn't take long to figure out what was going on. She had inserted into the WordPerfect file the bitmapped *picture* of what she had scanned in. I tried to explain, but she wasn't inclined to listen. I could only shake my head as she scanned it in again and kept on trying.

■ ■ ■

Hey, You Asked

Two of the leading personal finance software programs for small businesses are Quicken and M.Y.O.B. (Mind Your Own Business).

< 35 >

While working for a software store a couple of years ago, a telesales agent had this conversation.

Caller: Can you suggest the best home office accounting package?

Tech: In my opinion, Mind Your Own Business.

Caller: How *dare* you talk to me like that! I'll never do business with your company again!

■ ■ ■

Or Maybe It Was the Yellow-Haired One

Electronic Arts receives hundreds of calls about its CD-ROM games. One of them is called Midnight Stranger, a game where you roam around a city at night looking for people to interact with. A man called the company, saying he was having problems on Midnight Stranger . . .

Caller: This program Midnight Stranger is locking up on me.

Tech: At what point does it lock up?

Caller: I don't understand what you mean.

Tech: Does it lock up at the same point every time?

Caller: I still don't understand what you mean.

Tech: Does it lock up when you start Midnight Stranger, at the middle of the game, the end? Where? When?

< 36 >

Caller: Oh, oh. It locks up when you are at the girl's house and she's sitting on the couch.

Tech: OK, the brunette?

Caller: No, the dark-haired girl.

■ ■ ■

At Least It Wasn't the Ice Dispenser

From the logbook of a major computer company's tech-support rep:

Problem: Customer's important floppy disk is unreadable.

Cause: Wife had put disk on refrigerator door with a magnet to remind her husband to take the disk to work with him.

■ ■ ■

One Stressful Tech-Support Call

A friend of mine is a chief engineer at SuperMac, and he related this story to me. SuperMac records a certain number of technical-support calls at random, to keep tabs on customer satisfaction. By wild "luck," they managed to catch the following conversation on tape:

< 37 >

Some poor SuperMac tech-support agent got a call from some middle-level official from the legitimate government of Trinidad. The fellow spoke very good English, and fairly calmly described the problem. It seemed that a coup attempt was in progress at that moment. However, the national armory for that city was kept in the same building as the legislature, and there was a combination lock on the door to the armory. Of the people in the capital city that day, only the chief of the Capitol Guard and the chief armorer knew the combination to the lock, and they had already been killed.

So, this officer of the government of Trinidad continued, the problem is this: The combination to the lock is stored in a file on the Macintosh, but the file has been encrypted with the SuperMac product called Sentinel. Was there any chance, he asked, that there was a "back door" to the application, so they could get the combination, open the armory door, and defend the Capitol Building and the legitimately elected government of Trinidad against the insurgents?

All the while he is asking this in a very calm voice, there is the sound of gunfire in the background. The tech-support guy put the caller on hold. A call to the phone company verified that the origin of the call was, in fact, Trinidad. Meanwhile, there was this mad scramble to see if anybody knew of any "back doors" in the Sentinel program.

As it turned out, Sentinel uses DES to encrypt the files, and there was no known back door. The tech-support fellow told the customer that aside from trying to guess the password, there was no

< 38 >

way through Sentinel, and that they'd be better off trying to physically destroy the lock. The official was very polite, thanked him for the effort, and hung up.

That night, the legitimate government of Trinidad fell. One of the BBC reporters mentioned that the casualties seemed heaviest in the capitol, where there seemed to be little return fire from the government forces.

OK, so they shouldn't have kept the combination in so precarious a fashion. But it does place "My printer cartridge is clogged" complaints in a different sort of perspective, does it not?

■   ■   ■

Then What About Excel for Sega?

When I was working for a software company, I got a call from a customer wondering if we had WordPerfect for the Gameboy. "No," I said, "but I'll call you when it comes in."

Sometimes it's better not to ask any questions.

< 39 >

■ ■ ■

Sorry, Right Number

A customer called seeking help with her fax modem, which would no longer send faxes. Since she had a second phone line, the agent tried to walk her through the process while the customer was still on the line.

Agent:	Good. And now just choose the Fax command.
Caller:	OK. The fax dialog box came up.
Agent:	OK, do you know the number of a fax machine?
Caller:	No.
Agent:	Then just go ahead and put some inactive number in there so we can see what happens when it tries to dial. Then click on *Send*.
Caller:	OK. Oh wow, it's dialing! It's ringing.
Unknown Voice:	Hello? Hello, who is this?
Caller:	Oh no!
Voice (furious):	Who the hell is this?!
Agent:	Who is that?
Caller:	Oh my God! It's my grandfather and he's freaking out! How do I hang up?

■ ■ ■

The Blinking Ones Cost More

Australian Brett Wakeman spent some time on a help desk for PC-based software. One of his favorite calls was from a customer who he determined needed some changes to the AUTOEXEC.BAT file. Here's an excerpt from the conversation.

    Tech: OK, I'll need you to get out to the DOS prompt for me please.

    Caller: Oh, I don't think I've got one of those.

    Tech: What?

    Caller: I didn't order one when I bought the computer.

    Tech: No, sir, actually, the DOS prompt is part of the system software. All IBM PC users have one. Trust me: You've got one.

    Caller: Really? Great! I'd just better not tell my dealer I got one of those, or he'll want to bill me for it!

< 41 >

■ ■ ■

Turning the Other Cheek

One day, a friend of mine stood with his back turned to a table with a SparcStation on it. He leaned more and more on the table, until he was partially sitting on the Sun's keyboard.

When he stood up, we exploded laughing. In collaboration with the cursor keys and the Delete key, his butt had managed to change the *login:* prompt to say *login: assword:*

■ ■ ■

Punctuation. Period.

Consultant Keith Mabbitt learned, like thousands of techs before him, that nothing can be taken for granted in tech support.

While talking a customer through DOS over the phone, I wanted him to type *edit c:\autoexec.bat.* I was as clear as I could be. "OK, I'd like you to type the word 'EDIT,' press the space bar, type the letter C, type a colon"—at which point the caller asked what a colon was.

I explained that a colon is a punctuation mark that looks like a period above another period, and directed him to look for this key

< 42 >

on his keyboard. He seemed to take this in, but after several attempts, he still couldn't type the colon.

After fifteen minutes of this, I finally realized that he was trying to create a colon by typing a period, pressing the left arrow, and then attempting to type a second period over the first one.

■ ■ ■

The World's Dumbest Error Message

A friend of mine was trying to install Windows NT on a non-standard machine. Everything seemed fine until he actually ran Windows and a message told him that something had gone astray. I guess this could be considered an unrecoverable error:

No keyboard found. Press F1 to continue.

< 43 >

The Peripherals

"Peripherals" is computerese for all the junk you plug *into* your computer: printer, scanner, disk drives, keyboard, mouse, and so on. Each is a sophisticated, highly engineered machine unto itself—meaning it's equally as likely to confuse us, baffle us, and break down as the computer itself.

■ ■ ■

And Lock It, Too

A tech was taking his customer through the steps of inserting a floppy disk into his PC-compatible machine. Since the customer was a novice, the agent was taking no chances. He instructed the caller in the steps to inserting a floppy correctly, including pushing the disk in all the way and then closing the door on the disk drive.

< 44 >

Tech: Push the disk in all the way, and then close the door.
Caller: OK, hold on.

(Sound of phone being put down. Footsteps. Sound of the door to the room closing.)

■ ■ ■

The Ultimate Color Printer

     Tech: Hewlett-Packard Customer Service, can I help you?
Customer: Yes, I have a DeskJet that I need to have repaired.
     Tech: We make several different DeskJet models, ma'am. Do you know what model yours is?
Customer: It's a Hewlett-Packard!
     Tech: Yes, I know, but—OK, well, let's put it this way: Can you tell me if your printer is color or black-and-white?
Customer: Well, it's . . . beige!

■ ■ ■

Maybe *You're* Trouble

This report comes to us from a former technical-support specialist for a mail-order company. She got a call from a customer who wondered

< 45 >

if her new printer would absolutely, positively work with her Macintosh Performa. The printer was a StyleWriter II, ordered several months earlier. She also wondered if the CD she bought from the same company a year earlier would work on her Mac.

Tech: Yes, ma'am, the CD should work just fine with your Mac.

Caller: But it doesn't specifically say *my* Macintosh on the box.

Tech: What does it say?

Caller: Mac II and above.

Tech: It'll work. Your Mac is much more recent than the Mac II.

Caller: Oh, I just *know* I'll get in trouble.

Tech: Trouble?

Caller: Yes. I'm sure it won't work; that's why I haven't opened it. I just don't want to get in *trouble*.

Tech: Have you opened the printer?

Caller: No. I knew it wouldn't work either, and I didn't want to get in trouble.

Tech: How will you get in trouble?

Caller: Well, I won't be able to return them.

Tech: Ma'am, we are here to help you, and I will gladly stay on the line while you get the CD and the printer working.

Caller: No. If I open it, I'll get in trouble.

Tech: Who will give you trouble?

Caller: You will.

< 46 >

Tech: No, I won't. I want to help you get these things set up. They're doing you no good sitting in the box.

(At this point, her son can be heard in the background demanding the CD from his mother. He intends to try it. Lo and behold, he tries it, and it works.)

Tech: That's great news, ma'am. Now, why don't we get your printer working?

Caller: Absolutely not. If I take it out of the box, I can't send it back if it's defective.

Tech: But there's no way to tell if it's defective unless you take it out of the box!

Caller: No.

Tech: Ma'am. Why did you spend good money on these products if you're afraid to open them?

Caller: I don't want to get in trouble. I want to return the printer. I just know it won't work.

Tech: I'm sorry, but I can't authorize a return on a product if we haven't even *tried* to make it work!

Caller (upset): I just don't want it.

Tech: Ma'am. You ordered this printer nearly eight months ago. It is entirely outside of our warranty by now, which only covers defective items in the

< 47 >

first place. Please let me try to help you get it set up.

Caller: Oh, I just *knew* I'd get in trouble!

■ ■ ■

Included Free with Your Computer Purchase

An AST customer called to complain that her mouse was hard to control while it had its "dust cover" on.

"Dust cover?" asked the tech. Yes, the customer insisted.

Turns out the "dust cover" was the clear plastic bag the mouse came in.

■ ■ ■

Making Better Connections

While troubleshooting for printer problems with a customer, an agent noticed that simple tasks were taking an inordinately long time.

Tech: Ma'am, I couldn't help noticing that every time I ask you to try something, it takes an extra long time.

Caller: This computer has the *worst* design—it makes me *so mad!* Every time I need to use the mouse, I have to move my

< 48 >

desk back from the wall, *unplug* the keyboard, and connect the *mouse*. How *frustrating!*

Tech: Ma'am, the mouse plugs into the keyboard.

Caller: You're *kidding*. You've *got* to be *kidding!* Oh my God, I
just knew there was something wrong. I've been using it
this way for over a *month!*

■ ■ ■

Not All There

*Most often, a help-line agent is asked to provide technical infor-
mation. Every now and then, however, the job entails skills more suited
to a game of Charades. This call falls into that category. The setup: The
customer's CD was stuck in the CD-ROM drive, and the technician was
suggesting the famous Paper Clip Trick—in which a straightened paper
clip, carefully pushed into the tiny hole beside the CD-ROM drive, will
neatly push out the CD in last-resort cases. English, unfortunately, was
not the caller's first language.*

Caller: I do not have dis—popper cleep. It did not come with
computer.

Tech: No, it's not part of the computer.

Caller: I look in box again, but I not see dis popper cleep.

Tech: No, sir—ah, are you not sure what a paper clip is?

< 49 >

Caller: No, this is first time using computer.

Tech: OK, well, it's actually not a part of your computer. It's a—it's like, it's an office supply. It's a little piece of bent wire, a little piece of metal, that you might use to hold two pieces of paper together?

Caller: Hmm. Let me see. *(Sounds of packaging and rooting around.)* Because dis computer come with a *lot* of paper . . .

Tech: OK, no, it's not something that comes with the computer. It's just something you might have lying around the house. A paper clip—you'd use it to hold a stack of paper together? Do you know what I mean, sir?

Caller: Ah. Like a peh—pob—like a pad?

Tech: Ah, no, it's a—kind of—it's a piece of wire? Metal?

Caller: Mmmmmmm. *(Long pause)* So you think dis CD not come out because I am missing this kind of paper?

Tech: No, it's a paper *clip.* Is it—is there—do you . . . *(Floundering in agony)* OK, do you think there might be somebody there you could ask? If they know what a paper clip is?

Caller: Mmmmmm.

Tech: Do that. Then get a paper clip and call us back. Do you think you could do that?

Caller: OK. Thank you very much. Bye-bye.

< 50 >

■ ■ ■

Yeah, That'll Help

A customer was perplexed by the error messages that were appearing whenever he tried to print. The computer would say, *Looking for LaserWriter,* and then, after a while, *Can't Find LaserWriter.*

His solution: He turned the computer so that the screen faced the printer.

■ ■ ■

Tales from the Sex Line?

Having just purchased a Zip drive for my Mac, I was having trouble connecting it. After half an hour, I figured it was time to call Apple's hot line and make sure I was connecting the cables properly. Imagine my surprise when the phone was answered, "Hello, sexy! You've reached the *hottest* chat line in America . . ."

It seems that I dialed 800-S-*zero*-S-APPL instead of S-*letter O*-S-APPL, and I'd been connected with a very different kind of help line. I guess it really is true—Mac users have all the fun!

< 51 >

■ ■ ■

Have You Checked Your Brain Antenna?

A tech was trying to help a customer whose computer had a TV Tuner card installed. The problem, according to the customer: "When I turn on channel 21 and hit Enter, the computer says, *System Request: Not a DOS Disk in DF8* in a big banner across the screen."

The tech rep could not duplicate the problem, making him think that perhaps channel 21 itself was at fault. He asked the customer to look at that channel on a regular TV. Sure enough, the same thing was on channel 21 on all the televisions in his house!

Channel 21 was the local cable company's preview channel, and its computer system had gone down.

■ ■ ■

There's No Manual for the Shrink-Wrap, Either

We received an angry call from a woman who had just bought a new PC from us. She had set her whole system up without incident until she came across the mouse pad we included at no extra charge.

"Which side of the mouse pad faces upwards?" she demanded. Despite the brightly colored company logo emblazoned on the

< 52 >

smooth side of the pad, the woman scolded us for not including appropriate instructions.

■ ■ ■

Talk About a Clean Install!

Every time the customer put the system-software CD into his CD-ROM drive and started up, the computer would freeze or display an *FPU Not Installed* message.

The tech-support agent walked him through all the usual trouble-shooting steps. Nothing seemed to work. When all else failed, he suggested that the customer *clean* the CD. The customer called back, delighted.

"You were right!" he said. "There was *cheese* stuck to the bottom of the CD!" He wanted to let everyone at the tech-help desk know how thankful he was.

■ ■ ■

If General Motors Had a Help Line, Part 3

Tech: General Motors Help Line, how can I help you?
Caller: Your cars suck!
Tech: What's wrong?

< 53 >

Caller: It crashed, that's what wrong!

  Tech: What were you doing?

Caller: I wanted to run faster, so I pushed the accelerator pedal all the way to the floor. It worked for a while and then it crashed and it won't start now!

  Tech: It's your responsibility if you misuse the product. What do you expect us to do about it?

Caller: I want you to send me one of the latest version that doesn't crash anymore!

■ ■ ■

New! Handy Compact Size

A student at the university where I work kept having problems with one of his 5.25-inch disks, complaining that none of the computers on campus would read it. When he came in to see me about it, I assumed he didn't have his disk with him because he was carrying neither notebooks nor backpack. So I suggested that he bring in the disk later in the day.

"Oh, no, I have it right here," he said, upon which he took the disk out of his back pocket, unfolded it, and handed it to me.

< 54 >

■ ■ ■

We Won't Even Ask About the End Key

Another classic tech tale involves a man who called the computer company to complain that he couldn't get his computer, which came with a fax modem, to fax anything. The tech spent forty minutes walking the customer through troubleshooting steps before the actual problem came to light: The customer was attempting to fax a sheet of paper by holding it up to the monitor and pressing the Send key on his keyboard.

■ ■ ■

The Do-It-Yourselfer

The caller was having trouble with the cartridges in her ink-jet printer.

Caller: So then I bought a new cartridge, and it printed fine for about half a page.

Tech: OK.

Caller: Then it quit putting ink on the paper, so I figured something was clogging the cartridge.

< 55 >

Tech: That's right. You see—

Caller: Wait, let me tell you what I did. I figured the cartridge wasn't getting enough air through it, so I drilled a hole in the side of it—

Tech: You what?

Caller: I know, I know, I shouldn't have done that. Basically, I'm just calling to ask if I should just use paper towels to sop up all the ink in the bottom of the printer, or would it void my warranty to drill a hole in bottom of the printer to let it drain out?

■ ■ ■

The "Everywhere You Want to Be" Floppy

A customer brought in a Macintosh with a floppy disk stuck in the disk drive. Even pushing a straightened paper clip in the manual-eject hole would not eject the disk.

Upon disassembling the disk drive, I discovered why. The customer had a fondness for carrying Mac disks in his front shirt pocket. He had also put his Visa gold card in his front pocket that day. It had managed to lodge itself on the back of the disk by slipping under the metal shutter. The customer had inadvertently inserted the disk, Visa and all, into the drive.

And yes, to pay for the repair, he charged it.

< 56 >

■ ■ ■

The Elusive Hub

A frustrated neophyte called a computer service department because she did not know which end of a 3.5-inch floppy disk to insert into her computer.

>   *Tech:* The rectangular metal part goes into the drive first, and the round silver hub faces down.
> *Customer:* I don't see any round silver part!
>   *Tech:* Turn the disk over?
> *Customer:* Oh, there it is!

■ ■ ■

All That Fancy Terminology

>   *Tech:* OK, next I'd like you to hold down the Option key . . .
> *Caller:* There is no Option key.
>   *Tech:* On your keyboard, sir.
> *Caller:* I'm clicking up there in the white bar at the top, but there's nothing that says Option.
>   *Tech:* No, sir: It's on your keyboard.

< 57 >

Caller: What is the keyboard?

   Tech: Where you type things.

Caller: I don't type things up there in the white line! I use this thing with the letters on it.

   Tech: That's your keyboard, sir.

■ ■ ■

We've All Had Floppies Like That

It's not only computer technicians who get calls from hapless novices. Sometimes it's just friends helping friends—or trying to.

My friend just got a new Mac. One day, she called me up saying that she had been trying for half an hour to get her disk out of the computer. I asked her if she'd tried the obvious: dragging the disk's icon to the Trash can. Impossible, she said; the disk's icon didn't even appear on the screen.

Next, I told her to try the Command-Shift-1 keystroke. No good; the disk still didn't come out. I even had her stick a straightened paper clip into the tiny hole next to the disk drive. She tried that, but still nothing.

Finally, I went to her house to solve the mystery. We took the Mac apart completely, finally extracting the floppy drive unit.

< 58 >

It was empty. She had spent all day trying to eject a disk that wasn't there!

■ ■ ■

A Disk in Time Saves Nine

It's a good idea to be explicit when giving instructions to new computer users, as this tale from a support specialist indicates.

Caller: We need a technician out right away. We always put ten floppy disks in the machine for the daily backup!

Tech: What's the problem?

Caller: Well, we got nine disks into the drive, but we can't get the last disk in.

■ ■ ■

Talk About Spewing Pages

Tech: OK, let's print a test page now.

Caller: Let me go see if it prints out.

(Five-minute pause. Footsteps coming back.)

< 59 >

Caller: Sorry that took so long. I had to go throw up, but it printed fine.

■ ■ ■

Hardware Not Included

The teller of this tale was a sales engineer at a major computer retailer.

A customer called me up, saying that she had just bought a recordable CD-ROM, but no icon was appearing on her computer screen when she inserted a disc. I talked her through the process of SCSI address settings, termination, and the other usual suspects.

Eventually, I established that she had an internal (built-in) CD-ROM drive. In fact, she said it came already installed in her computer. Since no machines at the time came with a built-in *recordable* CD-ROM drive, my suspicions were aroused. Finally, I asked her to describe exactly what she'd bought from us.

Turns out she'd bought a blank recordable CD-ROM *disc*—not a CD-ROM *drive*. She was slightly embarrassed when I explained that to record onto that disc, she still needed to buy another $2000 piece of equipment.

< 60 >

■ ■ ■

A Better Mousetrap

An America Online technician filed this report:

A member called up with the usual connection problems. I couldn't help noticing that it was taking her unusually long to do the simplest task—such as selecting an item from a menu.

The member said that her cat had eaten her mouse ball, and she therefore had to move the cursor by putting her finger in the cavity where the mouse ball used to be and moving the rollers manually.

■ ■ ■

The Classic Cup Holder Story

When a Novell system operator sent out this story on the Internet in 1995, it became an instant Tales from the Tech Line *classic.*

Caller: Hello, is this Tech Support?
Tech: Yes, it is. How may I help you?
Caller: The cup holder on my PC is broken and I'm within my warranty period. How do I go about getting that fixed?

< 61 >

Tech: I'm sorry, but did you say a *cup holder*?

Caller: Yes, it was attached to the front of my computer.

Tech: Please excuse me if I seem a bit stumped; it's because I am. Did you receive this as part of a promotional, at a trade show? How did you get this cup holder? Does it have any trademark on it?

Caller: It came with my computer, I don't know anything about a promotional. It just says "4X" on it.

(At this point the Tech Rep had to mute the phone because he couldn't stop laughing. The "cup holder," of course, was the computer's CD-ROM tray.)

■ ■ ■

Fixed Keyboard or Bust

One of our strangest calls came from a secretary who was complaining that her space bar was sticking down at times. We sent a technician down to look at her keyboard; it worked fine when he tried it.

Puzzled, he asked the secretary to try it. Lo and behold, the insertion point began scooting across the monitor, exactly as though the space bar were being held down. After further checking, he no-

< 62 >

ticed that the secretary had a large bust, overhanging the keyboard, and at times touching the keyboard.

He solved the problem by raising the seat on her chair.

■ ■ ■

Don't All Mice Squeak?

Caller: I would like to speak to someone about a major problem we're having with our new system. The mouse doesn't work, and it squeaks horrendously!

Tech: Sounds like you do have a problem. Maybe the mouse has a bad ball.

Caller: I'm moving it around right now—can you hear that unbelievable noise?

Tech: Yes. I can't say I have ever heard that from a mouse before.

Caller: Yeah, and it gets worse if I move it across the screen faster!

Tech: Ah—what do you mean, "move it across the screen"?

Caller: You know, like push it from one corner of the monitor to the other.

< 63 >

■ ■ ■

They're Not That Floppy

The customer was having trouble opening the word processing files on his old floppy disks. The tech interviewed the customer at length, making sure the floppies hadn't been near heat, magnets, and so on. The customer denied subjecting the floppies to any such damaging forces.

Finally, he asked the customer to see if he could remember doing anything else to the floppies. The customer replied: "No, not really. I put a label on the diskette, roll it into the typewriter . . ."

■ ■ ■

And We Don't Sell Ether Nets, Either

"Daisy chain" describes an arrangement of equipment in which one gadget is plugged into the back of the next, one after another. Clearly, not everybody's aware of that definition, as this rep for a mail-order company discovered.

I sold an external CD drive along with a Zip drive to a customer who was fairly new at computers. She was going to connect both of those

< 64 >

devices to her desktop computer. I made sure that she bought the proper cables for these two devices. I tried to describe the hookup process at the time she placed her order, but it was too hard to explain the concept of an SCSI daisy chain over the phone. I waited until her hardware arrived, and then called to see if she was having any trouble getting them connected.

Her reply: "Well, it's not hooked up yet, but we'll be OK. My husband just ran out to CompUSA to buy a daisy chain."

I couldn't believe it. "And did he get one?"

"No," she said. "The salesman said they only have the PC version available right now, but they said they'd special-order a Mac one."

■ ■ ■

Going Sleeveless

In the ancient days of the eighties, floppy disks weren't the hard 3.5-inch squares they are today. Floppies were actually floppy, consisting of a 5.25-inch square enclosure containing the usual round sheet of magnetic material. Even those floppies, of course, weren't problem free, as Joe Bedard reports.

I work in the tech section at Alaska Computer Brokers. A man came in and said that he couldn't get his info off a couple of his floppies.

< 65 >

Of course, this was vital info that had taken the customer many hours to create. I'm thinking that a simple disk utility program would fix this man's problem. Five minutes tops. The man went on to tell me that all he did was follow the instructions in the floppy box.

"What instructions?" I asked.

"The instructions say that these floppies are preformatted," he replied, "and that you need to remove the plastic sheaths on them."

I said OK, thinking of the little worthless envelopes disks come in. The man then handed me two round black magnetic disks. He had ripped these poor floppies apart, slicing open the square protective casing to remove the actual naked magnetic disk, which he had then attempted to cram into his floppy drive.

■ ■ ■

But the Fonts Look Great

Another actual call from a major computer company's tech line:

Caller: Hello, I'm calling about my printer. It won't print.

Tech: Have you tried doing a test page?

Caller: Yes.

Tech: Exactly what does the printer do when you do a test print?

< 66 >

Caller: It feeds the paper through the printer, and it sounds like it's printing, but the page is blank.

Tech: Have you changed the printer ribbon?

Caller: Yes, I've tried four new ribbons.

Tech: Ma'am, I recommend that you take this printer to a local repair center. We can refer you to a local service provider, or you can check your Yellow Pages.

Caller: You'll have to refer me, young man. I can't check the Yellow Pages because I'm completely blind.

■ ■ ■

No, That Requires an Attachment

A customer called up the company that made her handheld scanner, complaining that it wasn't scanning correctly. After several minutes of hardware and software questions, the tech asked what exactly the person did to scan.

"Well," she said, "I just put it on the side of my head and dragged it down."

< 67 >

■ ■ ■

Maybe If You Change the Little Type Ball?

In the days before laser printers, your best bet for letter-quality printing was a daisywheel *printer—a printer that typed letters onto the page by slamming little metal plates with the characters formed on them against a ribbon. Seymour Dupa, working at a computer store, received this call.*

> *Tech:* Hello, can we help you?
> *Caller:* I'm having trouble with my Diablo 630 daisywheel printer.
> *Tech:* What kind of trouble?
> *Caller:* I can't get it to print out the graphics from my painting program.

■ ■ ■

Probably Stores Less, Too

When one of our computer labs upgraded from Apple IIe computers to Macs, one student came to me because she was having problems with the new computers. She had "reformatted" her 5.25-

< 68 >

inch disks by trimming them down with a pair of scissors so that they would fit into the 3.5-inch drives.

■ ■ ■

We're Working on That Feature

Caller: Hi, I'm having trouble with my printer.

Tech: OK, sir. What kind of computer do you have?

Caller: You need the computer?

Tech: Yes. Is it a PC or a Macintosh?

Caller: You mean you need a computer to make it print?

Tech: Ah, that's right. I mean, what are you trying to print from? What are you trying to print?

Caller: Well, I took this picture—

Tech: With a camera?

Caller: Right, and I'm trying to print it.

Tech: You mean the roll of film? What exactly did you do with it?

Caller: Well, you know, I opened up the printer and put the roll in there and closed the lid.

< 69 >

■ ■ ■

Safe Hex

The computer service tech where I work got a call from a secretary complaining that the floppy drive in her computer wouldn't work.

He went down to check it out, and found that she was putting the disks in with the clear plastic wrappers still on them.

He asked her why she was doing that. Her reply: "Well, I didn't want my computer to get a virus."

■ ■ ■

Format and Function

A client's hard drive developed problems; fortunately, as per our recommendation, he had bought a tape backup drive and religiously made backups of his data every day. But he called us because he couldn't figure out how to restore his data from the backup tapes—they all seemed to be blank. We tested his tape drive and his tapes, and they all seemed to work fine—except that, as he said, all the tapes were indeed empty.

Bewildered, I asked him to come into the shop and go through

< 70 >

the steps of backing up and restoring just to make sure he was doing everything correctly. As we watched, he launched the backup software, inserted one of his tapes into the tape drive, pulled down the Utility menu, and selected the Format command.

"What are you doing?" I exclaimed. "Format means Erase!"

Dumbfounded, the client pointed out that on the case of each tape, it says "THIS TAPE MUST BE FORMATTED BEFORE USE." Logically enough, he assumed that each tape must be formatted before *each* use—and had thus been methodically erasing each backup tape each time he put it into the drive.

■ ■ ■

But Shipping Is Extra

I received a call from a customer who had just received his repaired laptop back from us. He wanted to know how he should send the *box* in which it was shipped back to us.

He went on and on, saying how nice a box it is, and that it's very nicely padded. He couldn't imagine us not wanting to have it returned.

I told him he could keep it as a "gift."

< 71 >

The Screen

For most newcomers to today's miraculous machinery, the monitor, more than any other component, *is* the computer. This is where the computer's personality is exhibited, where the work gets done, and where the error messages appear.

■ ■ ■

So It's Not the Socket, Then?

Nils Hedglin was once called for help by a legal secretary, who told him that her monitor wasn't working. She asked if he'd please come over to her office to replace the bulb.

< 72 >

■ ■ ■

The New Jersey Computer Widow

The owner of Atlantic Computer Systems, a computer store in New Jersey, tells us about one computer widow who took things into her own hands. (A computer widow, of course, is a woman whose husband spends more time with his PC than with his spouse.)

Anyway, this particular woman took a low-tech approach to solving a high-tech problem. She grabbed a hammer and smashed in her husband's fifteen-inch color monitor.

No report on whether that New Jersey couple now spends more time together.

■ ■ ■

Monitor Stable, User Not

Formal education has no relationship to technical expertise. Two things tell us so: (a) eight-year-olds designing their own Web sites, and (b) this story.

We have a service contract at a local college. I got a call one day from a respected professor there, someone with "Dr." in front of his

< 73 >

name. He said that whenever he typed on the keyboard, the image on the monitor would shake. All sorts of monitor problems ran through my mind. He told me that the shaking occurred only when he typed.

Well, since it was a contract, I figured we'd better go see what was happening. I sent my tech over to the college. He called me about ten minutes after arriving and reported that he had found the problem.

It was not, in fact, the computer, the monitor, or the monitor image that was shaking—it was the *desk*. One leg was slightly shorter than the others, causing the entire tabletop to shake when the professor typed on the keyboard.

■ ■ ■

Let's Hope He's Kidding

An actual message posted on Apple's on-line tech-help bulletin board:

I have a small problem with my new Power Macintosh 7200. Everything works fine until I turn it on. Then the screen freezes; sparks fly out of my keyboard; my monitor spins around 360 degrees; green pea soup comes out of my floppy drive; and a hollow voice cries, *"You are doomed!"*

< 74 >

Pressing the Restart key has no effect. The only way I could stop this from happening was to burn down my apartment and move to a different city.

■ ■ ■

No, No, the *Other* Big Box

Many computers require that a video card be installed in the computer itself, into which you can plug a monitor. This often requires the help of a technician—and sometimes even the technician needs help.

Our computer store sent a new technician into the field to install a new video card. He had been gone for several hours; just when we started wondering what had become of him, he called in.

"OK, I've taken the monitor apart," he reported. "Now I just can't figure out where to install the video card!"

■ ■ ■

Cool But Not Refreshing

James Ng isn't a computer tech—he just plays one in his family.

< 75 >

One of my cousins was a die-hard computer game fan; he wasted hours of homework-time hours playing games. His parents had warned him on numerous occasions not to waste so much time playing, but since they were rarely home, my cousin usually got away with it. However, eventually his parents hit upon the idea to test the temperature of the monitor by touching it, thereby determining how long it had been on.

I told my cousin that I used to trick my parents by using a fan to blow down the heat. Shortly thereafter, however, he got caught and severely punished—and managed to destroy the monitor in the process. "What happened?" I asked.

"I thought cold water would cool the monitor faster than a fan," he told me glumly.

■ ■ ■

Pringle's Newfangled Monitor Jitters

Most of these tales were submitted by the nation's tech-support specialists. But sometimes the customer himself comes clean . . .

I thought my old computer was having some major problems one night—when I looked at the screen, I'd see it periodically jiggle. I ran Norton Utilities, I ran virus checker software; I just could not figure it out. I looked for electrical interference, changed power strips,

< 76 >

switched outlets, everything. My testing was made more difficult because the monitor shimmering was intermittent.

After thirty minutes of this, I called my older brother, who is a certified technician. He walked me through a bunch of things, and then he noticed that I'd been eating some chips during our conversation.

"How long have you been munching?" he said.

"About forty-five minutes," I replied.

"Stop munching," he told me. "Every time you chew something crunchy, the monitor appears to jiggle because of the vibrations in your skull."

He was right. Boy, was I embarrassed.

You should try it sometime. It really does jiggle!

■ ■ ■

Let's Reconsider That Name

Some of Apple's monitors are called Multiple Scan, *otherwise known as multisync; this term means that the picture can be enlarged or reduced for special purposes. Clearly, this caller had one very special purpose in mind.*

Tech: What product may I help you with?

Caller: It's the Apple fifteen-inch Multiple Scan monitor. We're

< 77 >

having trouble scanning. We put a piece of paper up to
the glass, but it wouldn't scan.

■ ■ ■

And Pull Down the Shades

Tech: All right. Now I'd like to quit any programs you're running, and close any windows you've got open.

Caller: Well, OK . . . There are only two windows here in the
basement, and they're both already closed.

Tech: No, no—the windows on your screen . . .

■ ■ ■

The High-Tech Chair-Accommodation Feature

I was helping a customer try to print from her new laptop. Early
in the call, the customer indicated to me that she had to get on the
floor for a moment. I didn't think too much of it, but later in the
call, when I asked her to try another step, she told me again that
she needed to get on the floor.

Now I was curious. "Ma'am, why is it that you keep having to
get down on the floor?"

"So I can see the screen," was the response.

< 78 >

I asked hesitantly, "Um, why don't you just tilt the lid of the laptop back farther so you can see the screen more easily?"

After a very quiet moment, I heard the caller say, "*Wow!*"

■ ■ ■

Where's the Remote?

Last week, I installed a computer for a coworker. It was the very first computer she had ever used. She called me early the next morning. She said her monitor was fuzzy-looking, and she wanted to know if she needed to buy an antenna for it.

I told her no, it was cable-ready.

■ ■ ■

How's That Again?

I work at the support hot line for a company that sells Unix systems. Customer calls are first handled by receptionists who determine the general nature of each caller's problem and then forward it to the specialists.

The receptionists attach a "headline" to each call so that the support analysts can decide whether a call is within their areas of expertise.

Unfortunately, the receptionists are not generally familiar with

< 79 >

Unix. Sometimes the receptionists mangle Unix in fascinating ways. Here are a few we've collected over the years:

"Getting a parody error."
"If terminal is off, can't get prompt back."
"Having a hard disfailure."
"Question about configuration of WoodPerfect."

Sometimes there's strange imagery involved. Picture this:

"System running in two time zones."
"Terminal is screaming."
"Cannot get into the library."
"Has a PC that knocks down all terminals."
"Runaway process boards."

There is some hardware we just don't support:

"Getting rat errors."
"Put in new version of VCR, has a couple of questions."
"Install wife terminal."
"Foot disk needs to be reformatted."

This is clearly not *a software problem:*

< 80 >

"Terminal burning up—smelling smoke."

Users may get a little fed up:

"Getting error message that says enough already."
"Can something be done? If so, how?"
"Is it possible to communicate with a Unix machine?"

Sometimes, you just wish you could respond . . .

"Users are getting bumped off and hanging up." *What presence of mind, replacing the handset just as they die!*

"Printer not talking properly." *Try starting it on the simple words: See Spot run . . .*

"Problem with PC going into the Unix box." *Tell that PC to STAY PUT!*

"How much swab space?" *Check the Q-TIP parameter.*

"Would like to kill a certain group of users." *Yeah, well, wouldn't we all.*

"System is hung for the last two days." *Sounds like a personal problem!*

"Question about braking when dialing in from a modem." *Calling from your car phone?*

"Does not see the boot." *Check the end of your foot.*

"Cannot get into Telnet." *Yeah, well, Telnet is pretty boring.*

< 81 >

"Constant memory vaults." *You're using too many JUMP instructions.*

"X's and O's on terminal." *How cute, it's telling you it loves you.*

"Terminal density is gone—cannot see screen." *Someone call a physicist—their system is losing its mass!*

"Bust fault and reset of system." *Can the hardware guy install a bra?*

"Questions on fox-based software." *Those animals really do understand relational databases!*

"Problem logging on to root, gets Chinese characters." *Oh, your console is upside-down.*

"Each time he accesses a dose, you have to reset the terminal." *Wow, man, the screen is breathing . . .*

"Kill process logs users off system." *It does tend to do that.*

"UPS DOWN." *And down is up, right, sir?*

"Wants to know how to do PCP over x dot 25." *Please, don't network under the influence.*

■ ■ ■

And Then Call an Electrician

User: Your software killed my monitor!

< 82 >

Tech: Pardon?

User: I installed your software and left the room, and when I came back my monitor didn't work!

Tech: Are you sure everything is still plugged in?

User: Do you think I'm stupid? I've already tried that!

Tech: Hmm. Hey, is your power socket controlled by a light switch?

User: Huh?

Tech: Did you turn off the lights when you left the room?

User: Uh . . . yeah.

Tech: Go turn the lights back on.

■ ■ ■

Help! Toasters!

The caller was concerned about occasionally seeing flying toasters on her screen. She wanted to know if this was normal. She was familiar with fish occasionally appearing on her screen, but thought something might be wrong when the flying toasters appeared.

I told her that the flying toaster is a normal phenomenon and inherent in her screen saver technology.

She started giggling uncontrollably and hung up.

< 83 >

■ ■ ■

Better Check Your Home Address Tonight

My department employed a beloved old VAX programmer who'd been there for years. For all his years on the VAX, he was occasionally a little clueless.

One day he came to my office, asking if I would look at some messages that came up while doing the shutdown. After he led me back to his cubicle, he walked in and sat at the PC—and *really* freaked out. "Now look at *these* messages!" he exclaimed. "These aren't the ones I had before! My God, everything's different—these aren't even my files!"

An irrepressible suspicion welled up deep inside me. "Let me ask you this, Bob," I said, pointing to the photo on the desk. "Is that your wife?"

"Well, no, dammit!" he said, even more perplexed. "Somebody's even rearranged my desk!"

I knew it: He had walked into his coworker's cubicle by mistake.

< 84 >

The Modem

The modem, of course, is the little box that connects our computers to the phone lines—and from there to the wonderful on-line world of cyberspace. Few inventions in the last twenty years have changed society so dramatically. Indeed, you can't open a newspaper these days without encountering the word "Internet." You can't E-mail a teenager without reading the word "Web." And you can't talk to a first-time modem user without hearing the word "Help!"

■ ■ ■

The Great AOL Ripoff

America Online is considered by many to be the easiest on-line service to use. But not for everyone, apparently:

Caller: I can't get your service to work. I'm really upset about

< 85 >

all of this. You're ripping me off, and I'm not going to
let you get away with it.

Tech: Well, what's the problem you're having?

Caller: Well, I set everything up like you told me to, and I
double-clicked on the Sign On icon and nothing happened.

Tech: Can you hear your modem dialing?

Caller: My what?

Tech: Your modem. The little device that lets your computer
talk to ours over a phone line.

Caller: Well, dammit, you didn't tell me I needed one of those.
You people are always trying to screw us with all of these
hidden costs!

■ ■ ■

A Very Different Area Code

A customer account specialist for PacBell, the California phone com-
pany, was handling a call from a customer who'd been trying to get
onto the Internet using PacBell's Internet service.

User: I know this is going to sound strange. But every time I
try to run the Internet, the police show up at my house!

Tech: The police?!

< 86 >

User: That's right.

Tech: Hmm . . . Let's look at the number you're dialing. What prefix have you added to the local Internet number?

User: OK, well, I have to dial 9 to get an outside phone line, right?

Tech: OK.

User: And then 11—

Tech: What?! Why are you dialing 11?

User: Well, I just moved here from Brazil. Don't I still have to dial the U.S. country code?

■ ■ ■

In-House Tech Support

We only have one phone line at my house. So my parents want me to put a sticker on the phone when I'm on-line using the modem.

So, one day, right after I get off, the phone rings. From her bedroom, before answering the incoming call, my mom yells, "Are you still on-line?"

< 87 >

■ ■ ■

Well, That's Success, Isn't It?

We've got a bulletin board as part of our tech-support service. Customers can log on, give themselves a password, and download useful items. Customers forget their passwords all the time, and such was the case when one gentleman dialed in and tried to log on. We happened to be working on the bulletin board at the time, so we watched with not a little amusement the following interaction between him and the bulletin board server:

```
    name: SMITH
password: BLOWJ*B
*** log on failed ***

    name: SMITH
password: BLOW J*B
*** log on failed ***

    name: SMITH
password: MONEY
*** log on failed ***
```

< 88 >

At this point, the gentleman gave up and called us a moment later to find out what his password was. We had already looked it up. It was "SUCCESS."

■ ■ ■

Must Be Around Here Somewhere

Tech support is hard enough without having to walk customers through Windows programs. The only thing harder is handling a Windows telecommunications program, as this poor tech had to do.

Tech: Ma'am, what kind of modem do you have?

Caller: Modem? I don't really know.

Tech: Well, is it internal or external?

Caller: I don't know . . . I found it, I found it! You want the name and model number?

Tech: Yes, please.

Caller: It says "Penshum" on the front panel!

Tech: No, ma'am, that's the computer. And it's "Pen-tee-um." Anyway, let's keep looking for the modem. Look around the computer. Do you see anything shaped like a small box near your computer?

Caller: Oh, that one! Yes, there's a little box right here. With disks in it. Is that the modem?

< 89 >

■ ■ ■

Simile Failure

Near the end of the three-month Internet course I teach, one of my students (a very bright M.D., by the way) approached me after class. He berated me for having provided incomplete information in the class about FTP—file-transfer protocol, which allows Internet users to download free software to their computers.

When I asked him what the problem was, he pointed to the paragraph on the syllabus that began, "The FTP service is like a public library."

This poor guy had spent three weeks trying to *return* the files he had downloaded from an FTP service!

■ ■ ■

Yes, But Is It 10 Cents a Minute?

A great trick for a modem is to open a terminal program and type AT13. The terminal program responds by displaying all kinds of information about the modem you're using—its brand, speed, and so on. When an America Online member called for help getting on-line but

< 90 >

didn't know what kind of modem he had, the tech rep tried to use that trick to good advantage.

>Tech: OK, sir, now that you have the terminal program running, I want you to type *AT13*, and press Return.
>Caller: OK, I'm doing it.
>Tech: What does it say now?
>Caller: It says *AT&T Data/fax modem 14–* Wait a minute, I see the problem right here. I use MCI, not AT&T.

■ ■ ■

Don't They Make an Adapter for That?

In the Web-browser software wars, of course, Microsoft and Netscape have made it common practice to make beta *(still-in-testing) versions of their Web software available, free, for anyone to try. Thus, this call reported by a computer teacher:*

>Caller: I downloaded Netscape according to your instructions. What a waste! I deleted it.
>Tech: Why?
>Caller: Because it said *Netscape beta.* My computer is a VHS!!

< 91 >

■ ■ ■

Well, That'll Make This a Little Harder

A tech at Netscape Communications received an E-mail from a customer. It said, "I can't receive any E-mail; I can only send it. I don't know how much good it will do, but here's my E-mail address."

Responding to the customer was made more challenging by the fact that he failed to provide his name or phone number—in a message that explained that he can't receive E-mail!

■ ■ ■

If General Motors Had a Help Line, Part 4

Tech: General Motors Tech, how can I help you?

Caller: Hi, I just bought my first car, and I chose your car because it has automatic transmission, cruise control, power steering, power brakes, and power door locks.

Tech: Thanks for buying our car. How can I help you?

Caller: How do I work it?

Tech: Do you know how to drive?

Caller: Do I know how to what?

Tech: Do you know how to drive?

< 92 >

Caller: I'm not a technical person. I just want to go places in my
car!

■ ■ ■

$49.95 Plus Shipping

I work at the computer store on a campus. A few weeks ago, we
had a customer call in and ask, "I'd like to buy the Internet. Do you
know how much it is?"

■ ■ ■

The Young and the Clueless

As part of our tech support we've got a bulletin board on which
customers can log on, give themselves a password, and download
useful items. One customer called us up saying that he had forgotten
what his password might be.

We looked it up; it was a woman's name. When I told him what
it was, there was a silence on the other end of the line.

"Sir," I asked, "are you OK?"

"Yeah," came the tearful reply. "It's just . . . that was my wife's
name . . . my ex-wife. We just separated."

< 93 >

In tech support, we generally like to think of ourselves as being able to come up with a response for anything. Not so in this case.

■ ■ ■

And Bill Clinton Wants My Performa

A customer called, claiming that the Secret Service had entered her house and bent the pins on her computer's modem. She said that they also messed with her computer so severely that After Dark no longer worked properly.

She then told me that the Secret Service took her computer away and replaced it with a fake one for a while. Now, she said, she has the monitor back but not the CPU. How does she know? Because her CPU never had a startup chime before, and now it does. The Secret Service was also responsible for her printer not working, she said.

I referred her to Hewlett Packard to troubleshoot her printer. They may have already solved the Secret Service problem, too.

< 94 >

■ ■ ■

Customer One-Liners

Actual quotes from actual customer calls:

Do I hit F and 8 at the same time?

I have about twenty-thousand megabytes on my hard drive.

OK, I have a C:backsplash.

I have 384,000 free contentious memory.

I have a cursing flasher.

Do you have 3.5-inch diskettes? No, I only have three of them.

I have Microword Soft.

Do you want a forward backslash?

This DOS program says I have insignificant memory.

It says one copy filed.

I've been having problems with Prodigy ever since I bought a modem.

A friend of mine gave me your software, and I'm missing one of the manuals.

I'm in the CONSYS.FIG file.

I have SETUP.EXERSIZE on my B floppy.

I have a scummy card in my system.

Why can't I call more than one BBS with one modem at a

< 95 >

time? This *is* a multitasking system, isn't it??

I've been using Windows for well over twenty years now.

I'm in 386 enchanted mode.

Memory? Is that the RAM stuff?

I just purchased a two-gig external hard drive for my computer. What do I need it for?

What kind of system do I have? It's an HP.

My modem can't see my Windows!

No, I'm sure I don't have an extensions conflict. I just checked, and everything is plugged in fine.

My computer says it just performed an illegal operation. Do I need to call the police?

I'd like a copy of the Internet, please. I brought a blank disk.

< 96 >

The Brain

The previous chapters of this book have explored the components of computers most likely to be baffling and bizarre. For tech-line call takers, however, the most entertaining cases are those in which the questionable component is the caller's *other* computer—the one inside the skull.

We must hasten to acknowledge, however, that very often it's not a lack of brainpower that causes the breakdown; in many cases, the computer user is actually demonstrating more imagination and logic than computer manufacturers were prepared for.

■ ■ ■

Too Many F Keys

Consultant John Roushkolb was trying to help a user install a new version of her Internet software, and told her to do a "find on TCP."

< 97 >

Caller: Find? How do you do that?

  Tech: Press Command-F, and when the Find dialog box comes up, type *TCP*, and then press the OK button.

Caller: Which F should I push?

  Tech: The one on the keyboard, ma'am . . .

Caller: Which one? They all have numbers on them.

■ ■ ■

A Hard Cell

This tech tale isn't about a computer, but it's priceless. The scene: a Radio Shack, one fine day in 1997.

Customer: I'd like to return this radio. It's broken.

  Clerk: Have you checked the batteries?

Customer: Yes, they're fine. I'm positive.

The clerk checked the batteries anyway. This made the customer furious, but the clerk told him them that it was standard procedure to check the batteries. Lo and behold, they were deader than a doornail. The customer, however, wasn't convinced. He picked up one of the dead batteries and showed the clerk the expiration date on it, saying: "But look! It says right here: "GOOD UNTIL NOVEMBER 1999!"

< 98 >

■ ■ ■

Look for the Label Union

A chemical-company computer expert reports:

The secretary in the area where I worked had recently acquired a new computer. She called me over in distress one morning, saying she was having problems getting a floppy disk into the drive. It would only go about halfway in and no farther.

I checked to see if there was a disk already in the drive—no—and also used a paper clip to see if somehow the drive had gotten into the down position. I was stumped . . . until I looked at her disk. Now, as most computer users know, self-stick floppy-disk labels are designed to wrap over the top of the disk and cover a small portion of the back as well as the front. This particular woman, however, had placed the label over the *entire front* of the disk, including the sliding shutter, essentially taping it shut. When she inserted the disk, the shutter could not slide, and the disk would not insert.

I found out she had labeled two entire boxes of disks this way.

■ ■ ■

Well, That Would Explain It

One evening on campus...

  Tech: Welch Hall computer assistant, may I help you?

Caller: Well, I was just typing along in WordPerfect, and all of a sudden the words disappeared.

  Tech: Hmm. So what does your screen look like now?

Caller: Nothing. It's blank; it won't accept anything when I type.

  Tech: Can you move the cursor around on the screen?

Caller: There isn't any cursor; I told you, it's totally dark.

  Tech: Does your monitor have a power indicator?

Caller: I don't know.

  Tech: Well, then look on the back of the monitor and find where the power cord goes into it. Can you see that?

Caller: Yes, I think so.

  Tech: Great! Follow the cord to the plug, and tell me if it's plugged into the wall.

Caller: I can't tell. I can't see back there.

  Tech: Even if you lean way over?

Caller: Oh, it's not because I don't have the right angle—it's because it's dark in here.

< 100 >

Tech: Dark?

Caller: Yes—the office lights are off. There's a power outage in the building.

■ ■ ■

Let's Not Be So Literal

Tech-line tales are the international language, second only to music and romance.

I run a small tech-support and consulting business here in Zurich, Switzerland. In one of my classes, I noticed that one of my students was inexplicably pressing his mouse up against the computer screen. I made my way over to his desk to ask what he was doing.

He pointed to the screen, where, sure enough, a message said, *Click the mouse here to continue.*

■ ■ ■

A Real Creative Artist

I teach courses at CompUSA. One of my students was an artist who had finally decided to do some of her work on a computer. She had gone out and bought all top-of-the-line equipment. In the class,

< 101 >

she was thrilled to learn about the Font Size menu; up until that point, she hadn't been able to figure out how to change the size of her type. For several weeks, she'd been typing in what she wanted, printing it out, scanning it in a different percentage enlargement, and finally pasting the scanned image back into her document.

■　■　■

Who Ya Gonna Call?

A very agitated woman called us and explained that her mother had died a few months ago. Lately, she had been noticing that all of her files, when viewed as a list, were displaying the date January 1, 1904. She said her mother had been born on January 1, 1904. The caller thought that perhaps her mom was trying to talk to her from the spirit world—through the Mac.

I tried to explain that this was not related to her mother. I told her that 1/1/04 is the Mac's default date stamp when its built-in battery dies, and that replacing the battery would make the correct dates show up.

She wouldn't believe me.

< 102 >

■ ■ ■

Please Enter Your PIN Number

The service manager for a store in Canada observed a client making a perfectly reasonable mistake.

One of our clients ordered a Macintosh Quadra, but she didn't want the built-in CD that comes standard on that machine. No problem; I took the CD drive out before I delivered it to the customer. However, I didn't have the bezel, the blank face plate, with which to cover the CD-drive opening. So I set the system up, gave the client a quick lesson on its ins and outs, and told her I'd be back in a couple of days to replace the bezel.

I returned two days later and opened up the computer to install the new bezel. Inside, lying on the circuitry and components, I found about a dozen Post-it notes. I asked the client about it. She told me that she had put them in there because the original CD face plate, with its long, slim slot, looked like one of those trash receptacles they have on the ATM machines.

< 103 >

■ ■ ■

And Wash It First, Please

And now, a true tale from a computer store. Picture, if you will, a teenage customer presenting a computer game he wishes to return.

"I'd like to return this game I bought yesterday."

I checked to see if all the disks, manual, warranty card, and so on were in the box. Then I noticed that the customer was wearing the free T-shirt that came packed in the box with the game.

"I'm sorry," I told him. "We can only accept returns if the entire package contents and packaging is returned in salable condition."

"Yeah, it's all there."

"Uhhh, but you're *wearing* the T-shirt that came with it ..."

"What? You mean I don't get to keep the shirt anyway?"

■ ■ ■

Good Thing I Didn't Say JCPenney

We join this technician in mid-conversation with a customer who wants to buy more software.

< 104 >

Tech: Well, sir, for that, I think you should probably just visit your local Egghead.

Caller: Yeah, I got me a couple of friends.

Tech: Actually, sir, I mean the Egghead software store.

Caller: Oh! I thought you meant I should find a couple of geeks.

■ ■ ■

Self-Esteem 101

A caller to a major computer maker was irate. "This damned computer," said the caller, "said I was bad, and it called me an *in*valid."

The tech had to explain, straight-faced, that the DOS responses *bad command* and *invalid* shouldn't be taken personally.

■ ■ ■

Well, It's Harder to Guess Than "Password"

I had a secretary with a three-letter password, which was required to turn the computer on. After a one-week vacation, she forgot her password.

Fortunately, I keep a master list of passwords locked in a file

< 105 >

cabinet, organized by building, room, and initials. Next to her three-letter initials was—her three-letter password. Need I say more?

■   ■   ■

The Terminator's Comeuppance

The software installer for a large health-care computer systems company had no idea what he was stepping into one fine spring morning, but his efforts at politeness backfired in a big way.

In order to complete a new software installation on the mainframes, I needed to have all the users off the system. Rather than just shutting it down abruptly, I thought I'd warn everybody that any tasks they were processing on the mainframe—"jobs," in computer lingo—would be interrupted. So I sent a message to all the terminals that said, *Please sign off by 5:15 P.M. If you do not sign off voluntarily, your job will be terminated. Thanks.*

About five minutes later, I received a call from the most irate ICU nurse I have ever talked to. She demanded to know who I was and who I worked for. I explained to her that I was employed by the hospital to install their new system. She ranted and raved that my message was the most obnoxious and rude message she had ever read—and then she hung up on me. I asked two of my colleagues to

< 106 >

read the message, and both of them thought I was quite polite. After all, I did say "please" and "thank you."

When I brought the system back on-line, I called the emergency room to make sure everything was working OK. The nurse who answered the phone informed me that all was well, but then nervously asked me if she was going to be fired.

I told her I didn't know what she was talking about. She then explained that all the nurses who had been on the system thought that my message meant that their *employment* would be terminated.

I sent out a message over the system apologizing. The next morning, I ran into the CEO and CFO of the hospital, who thought the whole thing was hilarious and took to calling me the Terminator.

■ ■ ■

I Have This Friend . . .

This call to a major computer company's tech desk came not from a customer, but from the manager of a computer store.

Tech: How can I help you?
Caller: Yeah, I've got a customer who wants to get her husband a present for his birthday, and I'm trying to help them out. Uh . . . do you know . . . um . . . where you can get,

< 107 >

uh, you know, something with a bunch of pictures of naked women on it?

Tech: Uh . . . no, I don't think I do.

Caller: Well, thanks anyways.

■ ■ ■

Detective First Class

I was a detective in the auto theft unit of a large suburban police department. Now, everyone knew that I had some computer experience (i.e., I wasn't scared of them). This, of course, made me an expert in their eyes.

So, one day I was sitting at my desk when the phone rang. My lieutenant was on the line, asking me to come down to the Burglary sergeant's office . . . they had a computer dilemma. I went down to the office; as I entered, I was presented with an amusing sight. A lieutenant, two sergeants, and four burglary detectives were all standing, staring at this little laptop.

These seven men informed me that the laptop had been stolen in the burglary of a major company a few weeks earlier. It appeared to be an inside job. The laptop had been found at a local pawnshop, but there were no leads in the case. Now the burglarized company was asking us to see if some of their really important files were still intact.

< 108 >

Now, these seven investigators were standing over the laptop, with no idea how to even turn it on. They moved back and let me sit at the desk. I turned the computer on and soon was checking the files. Meanwhile, the room slowly emptied of personnel.

I knew the burglary had occurred on October 14. Well, suddenly I noticed that there were two files made on October 15. And they were called "Résumé1" and "Résumé2."

I opened them up. Sure enough, the thief had used the stolen computer to make his résumé!

I walked out of the office and up to the seven investigators—and mysteriously gave them the thief's name, address, birthdate, phone number, and employment and educational history!

Epilogue: The thief pled guilty. My status as computer expert is now legend.

■ ■ ■

Helping a Canadian Oot

Over the phone, we were trying to help our customer figure out how to operate a program. Because this was a Canadian customer, the call was long distance, and the stress was high. Over and over again, we'd instruct our Canadian friend to press Control-A. But somehow, our communications were getting garbled; our customer was getting nowhere.

At last, trying to maintain our cool, we said, "OK. Just press Control-A, and tell us what happens."

Our customer, exasperated himself, replied, "OK. I've pressed Control, eh? And nothing happened, eh?"

■ ■ ■

Get Both for Best Results

A friend of mine has a daughter who had started college and wanted a computer on which to complete assignments. Her father suggested she call me for some advice on what to buy, since he knew I work with computers.

I spent a while with her on the phone, answering questions and explaining in simple terms the basics of RAM, applications, Windows, and so on. I thought she had a pretty good grasp of the fundamentals—until she asked, "Oh, one more thing. Which is better, hardware or software?"

< 110 >

■ ■ ■

See You Next Week

Veteran tech reps will tell you that only part of their job is technical. The rest is psychological, as this transcript shows. The rep has answered several questions about the caller's printer.

Caller: Wow, you know everything! How can I get my ex-wife to talk to me?

Tech: I'm sorry, sir. Unfortunately, that's a little bit beyond the service we provide.

Caller (laughs): Right, OK.

Tech: Well, maybe you can try to be a little more understanding.

Caller: Yeah, you're right. I will try. Thanks . . . Listen, can I have your direct line?

< 111 >

■ ■ ■

The Home Key Doesn't Work, Either

My friend Duane was on duty in the computer lab. He noticed a young woman sitting in front of one of the workstations staring at the screen, with her arms crossed on her chest.

After about fifteen minutes, he noticed that she was still in the same position—but now she was impatiently tapping her foot.

He asked if she needed help. She replied, "It's about time you showed up! I pushed the Help button over twenty minutes ago!"

■ ■ ■

Or You Could Just Unplug It . . .

David Schargel, president of Aportis Software, started out his career manning the tech-support phones. He has a pretty good idea why computers aren't easy for everyone.

I got a phone call from a frustrated elderly woman who was trying to turn off her Macintosh. I did what I could to talk her through the process. Over and over again, I calmly attempted to teach her how to use the Shut Down command (in the Special menu).

< 112 >

Tech: OK, Mrs. Speck, do you see the word "Special" at the top of the screen?

Caller: Yes.

Tech: OK. Now just point to that word, Special, and press down on the button.

Caller: All right, I'm doing that.

Tech: All right. So now do you see the list of commands? Including the one that says "Shut Down"?

Caller: No. All I see is that word Special and the gray screen.

Tech: You're pointing right at the word "Special"? And you're holding down the button?

Caller: Yes.

Tech: You've got your finger on the button, and you don't see the menu drop down?

Caller: When you say "the button," you mean the big button, right?

Tech: Uh . . . what do you mean, "the big button"?

Caller: I'm pressing the big button. With one hand. And with the other, I'm pointing at the word "Special." Right?

From there, it was only another five minutes before David realized what she'd been doing. For the entire call, she'd been pointing to the Special menu with her finger. And she had indeed been pressing the button. Not the mouse button—the big button. The spacebar.

■ ■ ■

Did You at Least Use Defrost?

The Apple Newton is a handheld computer meant to be easily packed and carried around. It's supposed to be rugged, but not this rugged.

Tech: How may I help you, sir?

Caller: Well, a few minutes ago I spilled coffee on my Newton. I shook off most of the moisture, but I still had some liquid under the display.

Tech: Well, is the unit operating properly now? Will it turn on? Can you get it to display your data?

Caller: I need to tell you one more thing. Since there was moisture under the display, I stuck my Newton in the microwave for thirty seconds to evaporate it.

Tech: . . .

Caller: Are you still there?

< 114 >

■ ■ ■

Maybe We Should Offer Towels, Too

An actual transcript from Apple's Assistance Center, which you can reach by dialing 800-SOS-APPL.

Caller: Yeah, I'm calling about my free towel?

Tech: Your what?

Caller: I received this pamphlet saying if I ordered one hundred labels, I could receive a free Snapple towel.

Tech: Sorry, did you say a free towel?

Caller: Yeah, I'd like to get my towel.

Tech: What number did you dial to get to me?

Caller: 800-SNA-APPL.

■ ■ ■

A Higher Learning Program

I work at the tech-support center for a big computer company in Silicon Valley. One day, I received a call from a woman who wanted some computer lessons but was having trouble finding a local training company. During our conversation, she asked me if I could pro-

< 115 >

vide her with training personally. I told her that I was in California and it would be a little difficult for me to come to Florida to do so.

Her response: "Well, I work in a topless bar and use the computer there. Is that a good incentive to make the trip?"

■ ■ ■

Calling All Names!

The management at my tech-support company had been increasingly annoyed that some of us techs occasionally failed to type the customers' first and last names into the database. In fact, one morning in particular, my E-mail brought a stern declaration from on high that my group wasn't typing in the last names nearly as often as some of the other groups, and that there was no excuse, and that we had to start typing them in at once.

The incredible thing was that my very next phone call went like this:

Tech: Tech Support, can I have your name please?
Roman: Zox.
Tech: Thanks. So is Zox your first name or your last name?
Roman: My first name.
Tech: So what's your last name?
Roman: Zox.

< 116 >

Tech: I'm really sorry, but I need your first *and* last name.

Roman: It's Zox.

Tech: Look, I apologize, but my boss is going to get very upset if I don't get both your names.

Roman: My name is just Zox. You know how Madonna has only one name? Well, I'm just Zox.

■ ■ ■

> ### Try 555-1212@usa.com

Not every tech-line tale is about a customer. Every now and then, there's a corresponding story of humorous miscues by the tech reps themselves, like this one.

When I was setting up a service call for my broken computer, the woman in Tech Support was getting my contact info. She asked if I had another way of being reached other than by the phone number I gave her. I said that I could be reached by E-mail. She asked for my E-mail address. I gave it to her. Then, she wanted the *phone number* for my E-mail address.

Instills confidence, doesn't it?

< 117 >

■ ■ ■

Pleasure Doing Business with You

One day I received a call from an elderly woman who wanted to pay her local utility bill. I told the woman that she had reached a computer company, and that she had probably dialed the wrong number. I fully expected that she would acknowledge her error and that this would be the end of the call.

Much to my surprise, she countered: "Young man, don't tell me where I've called. I dial this number every week, and you can't tell me that I cannot pay my bill through this number!"

I was stunned. I repeated my assertion that she had reached the wrong number. Still, she wouldn't budge. She had dialed the right number, and come hell or high water, she was going to talk to someone who could help her.

I was exasperated, but being the quick-thinking employee that I am, I finally said, "My mistake, ma'am, you are correct. You have indeed dialed PG&E. If you just tell me the amount on your bill, I'll enter it into our records here." I made some keyboard noises in the background, trying to sound as official as possible. "You're all set here, ma'am. You can just mail your check in to us."

There was a pause on her end. Then: "Could you give me your address so I can mail my check?"

< 118 >

Uh-oh—caught! But wait—an idea. "Uhhhh, ma'am? Our address should be right there on your bill."

"Oh yes, you're right. Thank you, young man."

■ ■ ■

You Should Hear About *My* Day, Pal

It had been an unusually easy day of phone calls at this computer company's tech-support desk. Everything was quiet—too quiet—when . . . the phone rang.

Tech: Thanks for calling. How may I help you?

Caller: I've been trying to get through to you all day.

Tech: I apologize, sir. Were you on hold long?

Caller: No, it wasn't that. It was that all day, every time I picked up the phone, all I could hear was the hard drive. And no, I don't have a modem.

Tech: That's very odd. Is there something I can help you with now?

Caller: Well, that's not the only thing that's been weird. Today, my garbage disposal has been turning on by itself when I walk by it. Now my computer won't shut down.

< 119 >

> *Tech:* So, what exactly happens when you choose the
> Shut Down command?
>
> *Caller:* It acts like it's going to shut down, goes all the
> way to a black screen, then starts back up, except
> now I have to enter three passwords to get to
> the desktop. Before I only had to enter one.
>
> *Tech (kidding):* Ah, did any UFOs come by last night?
>
> *Caller:* Ahhh, no . . . but I *did* wake up on the floor.

■ ■ ■

Tech-Support Graffiti

*Spend too long answering tech-support calls, and you may start to
lose a few brain cells. Spend a lot of time with especially exasperating
customers, and you start to build up a few vitriolic thoughts. Here are
some of the wittier ways fed-up tech reps express such forbidden
thoughts—in support-center bathroom stalls, in intra-office E-mail, and
in conversation.*

SO MANY USERS, SO FEW GRENADES
Hit any user to continue.
Problem: Loose nut behind the keyboard.
Problem: Needed to turn up User Brightness knob.
Problem: PBKC. (Problem Between Keyboard and Chair.)

< 120 >

■ ■ ■

That's Classified, Sir

Tech: Good afternoon, my name is Larry. May I have your name, please?

Caller: I'm afraid I can't tell you that.

Tech: You can't tell me your name?

Caller: Due to the nature of my business, no, I can't.

Tech: OK, well, what can I do for you today?

Caller: The computer has a problem.

Tech: OK, can you be more specific?

Caller: I'm sorry, but because of what we do, I can't be any more specific than that.

Tech: I'm sorry, sir, but unless you tell me what the problem is, I can't help you.

Caller: OK, thanks. *(Hangs up.)*

■ ■ ■

No, But We Can Take a Mole Off Him

A customer called our desktop publishing outfit and wanted a poster made from a color slide. It was a picture of the caller's re-

< 121 >

cently deceased father with a couple of his fishing buddies in a boat. The caller mentioned there was a slight problem: In the picture, her father's back was to the camera. She wanted our photo expert to flip the negative so you could see his face.

When we explained that this would only provide a mirror image of the back of his head, she became irate. She screamed into the phone: "If you can take the pimples off those glamour girls, why can't you put a face on my father?"

■ ■ ■

More Information, Please

Caller: Yeah. About how far is it to your place from my house?
Tech: How far . . . ?
Caller: Well?
Tech: Well, sir, to tell you that, I sort of have to know where your house *is*.
Caller: What do you mean?
Tech: Sir, tell me where you live, and I'll tell you how far my place is.
Caller: I'm by Exit 4.
Tech: OK. I'd say eight miles. All right?
Caller: Yes. Thanks.

< 122 >

■ ■ ■

We'll Stop It, Then

Caller: I'm a consultant and I have a question about the RAM in a Macintosh.

Tech: OK.

Caller: It says here there's eight megabytes of RAM soldered onto the board. Why?

Tech: Well, so you can use the machine right out of the box. Without having to install additional RAM.

Caller: But in the DOS world, nobody does that. The machine won't boot unless you add RAM.

Tech: Well, we like to save our customers the trouble of buying and installing memory.

Caller: I don't like that. It's too different. I think it's a bad idea.

■ ■ ■

Then Charge Him for Motherhood

A customer called this tech rep, saying that she had just bought a memory upgrade card. She was calling to find out if it would work in her new computer.

< 123 >

Tech: Yes, that memory module should work fine.

Caller: Thank you. I just wanted to make sure before I took it to my son and had him install it.

Tech: Is your son an authorized service center for our computers?

Caller: Yes. He owns a computer store.

Tech: Just out of curiosity, why didn't you purchase this memory upgrade from him?

Caller: Because his prices are too high.

■ ■ ■

The Call Is in the Mail

One of our techs got a call from a demanding customer: No matter how detailed our tech's explanation was, it just wasn't detailed enough for this fellow. After forty minutes, our tech decided to give up and let someone else step up to bat.

Tech: I'm going to refer this to a senior technician. He'll call you in five minutes.

Caller: But that won't work! There's a three-hour time difference, and I won't be here in three hours.

< 124 >

Later, when the tech was telling this story to the rest of us, someone suggested that she should have responded: "Oh, but he already called you three hours ago—the call should be coming through any minute now!"

< 125 >

About the Author

David Pogue is the back-page columnist for *Macworld* magazine, the author of fifteen computer books (including the million-copy seller *Macs for Dummies*), a novelist (*Hard Drive*, a *New York Times* "Notable Book of the Year"), a conductor (and coauthor of *Opera for Dummies* and *Classical Music for Dummies*), and personal computer teacher to Mia Farrow, Carly Simon, Harry Connick Jr., Stephen Sondheim, and others. His other computer-humor books from Berkley include *The Great Macintosh Easter Egg Hunt* and *The Microsloth Joke Book*. He can be reached by E-mail (*pogue@aol.com*) or by Web page (*www.pogueman.com*).

< 127 >